Guitar
Exam Pieces

ABRSM Grade 1

Selected from the syllabus

from **2019**

Gary Ryan
Guitar consultant

Anthony Burton
Footnotes

Name

Date of exam

The code to download audio recordings of all pieces on the Grade 1
Syllabus is printed on the inside back cover.

First published in 2018 by ABRSM (Publishing) Ltd,
a wholly owned subsidiary of ABRSM, 4 London Wall Place, London EC2Y 5AU, United Kingdom

© 2018 by The Associated Board of the Royal Schools of Music
Distributed worldwide by Oxford University Press

Music origination by Moira Roach
Cover by Kate Benjamin & Andy Potts, with thanks to Brighton College
Printed in England by Caligraving Ltd, Thetford, Norfolk, on materials from sustainable sources.
P16072

Contents

Other pieces for Grade 1

茉莉花　Mo Li Hua

Jasmine Flower

Arranged by Peter Batchelar

Trad. Chinese

'Jasmine Flower' is a popular Chinese folk song, often performed on major public occasions such as the 2008 Beijing Olympic Games. The words praise the fragile beauty of the flower. The melody, in the typically Chinese pentatonic (five-note) scale, was first printed in a Western book in 1804. It was reproduced on a mechanical musical box brought back from China around 1900 by the Italian aristocrat Baron Fassini. Having heard the tune played on this musical box, Giacomo Puccini used it extensively in his last opera, *Turandot* (1926), which is set in Beijing.

On the bridge of Avignon

Sur le pont d'Avignon

Arranged by Richard Wright

Trad. French

'Sur le pont d'Avignon' is a well-known traditional dance-song from France, with the chorus:

Sur le pont d'Avignon	On the bridge of Avignon
On y danse, on y danse.	people dance, people dance.
Sur le pont d'Avignon	On the bridge of Avignon
On y danse tous en rond.	people dance in a circle.

The famous Saint Bénezet bridge in the southern French town of Avignon, built in the late 12th century, no longer crosses the river Rhône: only four arches at one end of it have survived.

Gaillarde Passemaize

A:3

Arranged by Helen Sanderson

Claude Gervaise
(*fl* Paris, 1540–60)

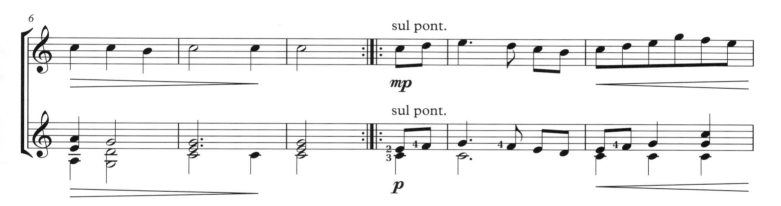

Claude Gervaise was a French musician of the mid-16th century who edited, arranged and composed four of a series of six volumes of dance music for instrumental ensemble, entitled *Danceries*. The sixth volume, published in 1555, which Gervaise composed himself, includes a 'Pavanne passemaize et Gaillarde'. The title indicates a pairing, typical of the period, of a duple-time pavane and a livelier triple-time galliard, both of them with harmonies resembling the chord scheme known in the Renaissance as the 'passamezzo'. This is an arrangement for two guitars of the Gaillarde. **In the exam, the candidate should play part I.**

B:1

Ecossaise

No. 5 from *24 pièces*, Op. 121

Arranged by Richard Wright

Ferdinando Carulli
(1770–1841)

Ferdinando Carulli, born in Naples in southern Italy but for many years based in Paris, was a famous guitarist, a pioneer of the six-string guitar and its use in a solo role. He also composed much music for his instrument. His Opus 121, which was published in Germany around 1825, or perhaps earlier, consists of 24 short pieces, mostly in dance rhythms. This one, presented here in a simplified version, is an Ecossaise, or Scottish dance, a popular genre in the early 19th century.

March

No. 19 from *Introduction à l'étude de la guitare*, Op. 60

B:2

Arranged by Richard Wright

Fernando Sor
(1778–1839)

Fernando Sor was one of the most celebrated concert guitarists of his time. He was born in Barcelona, and later lived and worked in Madrid, Paris and London. Having received an all-round musical education, he composed operas, ballets, orchestral works and songs as well as a great deal of guitar music. His *Introduction to the Study of the Guitar*, published in Paris shortly before his death, is a collection of 25 pieces arranged in ascending order of difficulty. No. 19, given here in a simplified adaptation, is in quick march time.

I vow to thee, my country

B:3

Arranged by Bridget Mermikides

Gustav Holst
(1874–1934)

This well-known melody was originally a theme in 'Jupiter, the bringer of Jollity', from the orchestral suite *The Planets*, written between 1914 and 1916 by the British composer Gustav Holst. In 1921, Holst was asked to make a song setting of 'I vow to thee, my country', a patriotic poem by the late diplomat Sir Cecil Arthur Spring Rice. He fitted the poem to a slightly adapted version of his 'Jupiter' tune. Later, in 1926, Holst arranged the song as a hymn for the hymn book *Songs of Praise*, and it became widely known in this form. Since 1991, it has reached a different audience as 'The world in union', the theme song of international rugby union. **In the exam, the candidate should play part I.**

Spanish Knights

James Longworth (born 1961)
and Nick Walker (born 1964)

This piece comes from the *Guitar Basics* series for beginners, written by two London-based composers and teachers, James Longworth and Nick Walker. It hints at the Spanish idiom of much music written for the guitar. The composers say about it: 'We were inspired to compose this piece by reading the famous story of the old and proud Spanish knight Don Quixote. Wearing a battered suit of armour, he sets out in search of adventure across the plains of La Mancha on his plodding and faithful horse Rocinante.' The metronome marking, dynamics and note on beat 1 of bar 25b (the second-time bar) have been added by the composers for this edition.

Underground Sound

Gary Ryan
(born 1969)

Gary Ryan is a well-known British guitar soloist and teacher; he is assistant head of strings and guitar professor at the Royal College of Music in London. The title of this specially written piece, he says, refers to the fact that much of the melodic interest is given to the thumb in the bass, 'with many of the notes on ledger lines "underground" below the stave'. He also notes that the piece uses the pentatonic (five-note) scale, requiring the use of only the second and third fingers of the left hand. Occasional syncopations give it 'a slight rock feel' (though the quavers should not be swung).

© 2018 by The Associated Board of the Royal Schools of Music

Somethin' Stupid

Arranged by Richard Wright

C. Carson Parks
(1936–2005)

'Somethin' Stupid' is a song in which the singer regrets spoiling a date 'by saying something stupid like "I love you"'. It was written by the American singer Clarence Carson Parks, and recorded by him as a duet with his wife Gaile Foote — as Carson and Gaile — in 1966. The following year, a recording by Frank Sinatra with his daughter Nancy went to the top of the American charts. There have been other versions since then, including one by Robbie Williams and Nicole Kidman in 2001, a No. 1 hit in the UK. This arrangement presents the melody line with a guitar accompaniment in a repeated rhythm. **In the exam, the candidate should play part I.**